TOP TIPS FOR GROWING YOUR STARTUP ON SOCIAL MEDIA.

CHRIS JOSH

Copyright © 2024 by Chris Josh

All rights reserved. No part of this book may be reproduced, stored in a retrieval system, or transmitted, in any form or by any means, electronic, mechanical, photocopying, recording, or otherwise, without the prior written permission of the author, except in the case of brief quotations embodied in critical reviews and certain other noncommercial uses permitted by copyright law.

TABLE OF CONTENT

INTRODUCTION 7

CHAPTER 1: BUILDING A SOLID FOUNDATION 10

- Defining Your Brand Identity 12

- Creating an Engaging Brand Story 16

- Choosing the Right Social Media Platforms for Your Startup 21

- Setting SMART Goals for Social Media Success... 26

CHAPTER 2: CRAFTING COMPELLING CONTENT 32

- Developing a Content Strategy Aligned with Your Brand 34

- Mastering Visual Content: Graphics, Images, and Videos............................... 39

- The Power of Storytelling in Captivating Your Audience.. 45

- Utilizing User-Generated Content for Authenticity 51

CHAPTER 3: OPTIMIZING YOUR SOCIAL MEDIA PROFILES................... 57

- Crafting an Irresistible Profile Bio...... 59

- Designing Eye-Catching Visuals for Profile Elements 64

- Leveraging Features and Settings for Maximum Visibility 70

- Maintaining Consistency Across Platforms... 76

CHAPTER 4: STRATEGIC ENGAGEMENT AND COMMUNITY BUILDING 82

- Building and Nurturing an Engaged Community 84

- Effective Use of Hashtags and Trend Participation 91

- Creating Contests and Giveaways to Boost Engagement 98

- Leveraging Social Listening for Customer Insights 105

CHAPTER 5: INFLUENCER COLLABORATIONS AND PARTNERSHIPS 113

- Identifying and Approaching Relevant Influencers 115

- Negotiating Successful Partnerships . 122

- Maximizing the Impact of Influencer Marketing 130

- Measuring ROI and Evaluating Influencer Performance 137

CONCLUSION 145

INTRODUCTION

Welcome to "Top Tips for Growing Your Startup on Social Media," your ultimate guide to navigating the dynamic landscape of digital platforms and propelling your startup to new heights. In the fast-paced world of entrepreneurship, establishing a robust presence on social media is no longer just an option—it's a necessity. This book is crafted to be your compass, steering you through the intricacies of leveraging social media to foster brand awareness, engage with your target audience, and drive sustainable growth.

In today's competitive business environment, startups face the dual challenge of standing out amidst the digital noise and building authentic connections with their audience. "Top Tips for Growing Your Startup on Social Media" is designed to empower entrepreneurs with actionable strategies, insider insights, and proven techniques to not only survive but thrive in the crowded social media landscape. Whether you're a fledgling startup or an established business looking to enhance your online presence, this book provides a roadmap to success.

Drawing on a wealth of industry expertise and real-world examples, this guide covers a spectrum of topics, from crafting compelling content and optimizing your social media profiles to mastering the art of influencer collaborations and deciphering analytics for strategic decision-making. Each chapter is a treasure trove of practical advice, distilling complex concepts into digestible tips that can be implemented immediately.

As we embark on this journey together, you'll gain a deeper understanding of the nuances of each major social media platform, ensuring that your startup not only adapts but thrives in this ever-evolving digital landscape. Let "Top Tips for Growing Your Startup on Social Media" be your companion on the road to social media success, offering insights that will empower you to elevate your startup to new heights in the digital age.

9 | Top tips for growing your startup on social media.

CHAPTER 1: BUILDING A SOLID FOUNDATION

Welcome to the foundational chapter of "Top Tips for Growing Your Startup on Social Media" — a critical starting point on your journey to digital success. In the world of social media, laying a solid foundation is akin to constructing a sturdy building; without it, the structure is prone to instability. This chapter is dedicated to helping you build a robust foundation for your startup's presence on social media platforms.

In "Building a Solid Foundation," we delve into the fundamental aspects that set the stage for your social media success. From defining your brand identity to choosing the right platforms and establishing achievable goals, this chapter provides a comprehensive guide to ensure that your startup's entry into the digital realm is strategic and impactful.

First and foremost, we explore the intricate process of defining your brand identity. We'll uncover the essence of your startup, helping you articulate a unique value proposition that resonates with your target audience. Once your brand identity is crystal clear, we move on to the crucial task of crafting a compelling brand story — a narrative that not only communicates your mission but captivates the hearts and minds of your audience.

Choosing the right social media platforms is the next crucial step in this journey. We'll navigate through the plethora of options, guiding you in making informed decisions based on your target demographic, industry trends, and the nature of your products or services. With these decisions made, we'll then delve into the art of setting SMART goals specifically tailored for social media success.

As we embark on this exploration of foundational principles, remember that well-established groundwork is the key to sustained growth. By the end of this chapter, you'll possess the insights and strategies needed to lay a solid foundation that will support and propel your startup's social media presence to new heights. Let's build together, ensuring that every subsequent effort in this book stands on a firm and strategic base.

- Defining Your Brand Identity

Defining your brand identity is a pivotal step in creating a distinct and memorable presence on social media. Your brand identity is more than just a logo or a color scheme; it encompasses the values, personality, and unique elements that set your startup apart in the crowded digital landscape. In this section, we comprehensively discuss the key components and strategies for effectively defining your brand identity.

1. **Understanding Your Mission and Values:**

   - Start by articulating your startup's mission and core values. What is the purpose behind your business, and what principles guide your decision-making? A clear understanding of these foundational elements provides a roadmap for shaping your brand identity.

2. **Identifying Your Target Audience:**

   - Know your audience inside out. Define your ideal customer personas, understanding their needs, preferences, and pain points. Tailoring your brand identity to resonate with your target audience fosters a deeper connection and engagement.

3. **Crafting a Unique Value Proposition:**

   - Differentiate your startup by articulating a unique value proposition. Communicate what sets your products or services apart from the competition, emphasizing the benefits your audience gains from choosing your brand.

4. **Expressing Brand Personality:**

   - Define the personality traits that embody your brand. Is your brand playful, professional, innovative, or authoritative? This personality should be consistent across all communication channels, creating a cohesive and recognizable brand image.

5. **Creating a Memorable Visual Identity:**

   - Visual elements play a crucial role in brand recall. Develop a visually appealing logo, choose a distinct color palette, and establish consistent typography. These elements should align with your brand personality and resonate with your target audience.

6. **Consistency Across Platforms:**

- Maintaining a consistent brand image across all social media platforms is essential. From profile pictures to cover photos and content style, consistency builds trust and reinforces your brand identity in the minds of your audience.

7. **Storytelling Through Content:**

- Narratives are powerful tools for conveying your brand identity. Share your journey, milestones, and customer success stories. Crafting a compelling brand story adds depth and relatability to your identity, making it more memorable.

8. **Feedback and Iteration:**

- Be open to feedback from your audience. Monitor responses to your content, engage in conversations, and adapt your brand identity based on insights. The iterative process ensures that your brand remains relevant and resonant over time.

9. **Monitoring Competitors:**

- Analyze how competitors present their brand identity. Differentiation is key, and understanding what others in your industry are doing can inform strategic decisions about your own brand identity.

Defining your brand identity is an ongoing process that requires introspection, market awareness, and adaptability. As you progress through this journey, remember that a well-defined brand identity is the cornerstone upon which a successful social media presence is built.

- Creating an Engaging Brand Story

In the realm of social media, where attention spans are fleeting and competition is fierce, a compelling brand story is a potent tool to captivate audiences, foster connection, and differentiate your startup. Your brand story is more than a narrative; it's a living, breathing entity that communicates the essence of your business. In this comprehensive exploration, we delve into the key elements and strategies for creating an engaging brand story that resonates with your audience.

1. **Origin and Founding Narrative:**

   - Begin by narrating the origin of your startup. Share the story of how it all began, the challenges faced, and the vision that propelled your venture forward. This founding narrative humanizes your brand, making it relatable and authentic.

2. **Defining Moments and Milestones:**

   - Highlight pivotal moments and milestones in your journey. These could be product launches, breakthroughs, or significant achievements. Incorporating these milestones into your brand story builds a sense of credibility and showcases your progression.

3. **Customer-Centric Narratives:**

   - Infuse your brand story with narratives that center around your customers. Share testimonials, success stories, and experiences that demonstrate the impact your products or services have had on individuals. This not only humanizes your brand but also establishes a connection with your audience.

4. **Values and Beliefs:**

   - Clearly articulate the values and beliefs that underpin your startup. Expressing a commitment to social responsibility, sustainability, or other ethical considerations adds depth to your brand story and resonates with consumers who align with these values.

5. **Building Character and Persona:**

   - Develop a distinct character and persona for your brand. Whether it's a charismatic founder, a team of passionate individuals, or a mascot, giving your brand a recognizable personality enhances its storytelling potential and makes it more memorable.

6. **Emotional Resonance:**

- Emotions are powerful motivators. Craft your brand story to evoke emotions that align with your messaging. Whether it's joy, inspiration, or empathy, an emotionally resonant story creates a lasting impact on your audience.

7. **Consistency Across Platforms:**

- Ensure that your brand story is consistently communicated across all social media platforms. Whether through written content, visuals, or video, maintain coherence in how your narrative is presented, reinforcing the central themes of your brand story.

8. **Interactive Elements:**

- Foster engagement by incorporating interactive elements into your brand story. Polls, quizzes, and user-generated content can turn your narrative into a conversation, encouraging active participation from your audience.

9. **Adaptability and Evolution:**

- A brand story is not static. It should evolve alongside your startup. Embrace adaptability, incorporating new chapters, and showcasing growth. This ongoing narrative reinforces the dynamic nature of your brand.

10. **Multimedia Storytelling:**

- Utilize a variety of mediums for storytelling. Combine written content with visuals, videos, and graphics to create a multimedia narrative that caters to diverse audience preferences and enhances engagement.

Crafting an engaging brand story requires a deep understanding of your startup's identity and a creative approach to narrative. By weaving a compelling tale that resonates with your audience, your brand story becomes a powerful asset in building a loyal and connected community on social media.

- Choosing the Right Social Media Platforms for Your Startup

Selecting the appropriate social media platforms is a pivotal decision that significantly influences the success of your startup's online presence. Not all platforms are created equal, and each caters to a unique audience with distinct preferences and behaviors. In this comprehensive discussion, we explore the key considerations and strategies for choosing the right social media platforms to maximize your startup's visibility and engagement.

1. **Know Your Target Audience:**

   - Understanding your target audience is the cornerstone of platform selection. Different demographics favor different platforms. Research and analyze the age, interests, and online behaviors of your audience to identify where they are most active.

2. **Platform Demographics and Features:**

   - Each social media platform has its demographics and features. Facebook, for instance, has a broad user base, while Instagram and Snapchat attract younger audiences. Evaluate the unique features of platforms, such as Instagram's visual focus or LinkedIn's professional networking, to align with your brand and content.

3. **Set Clear Objectives:**

- Define your social media objectives before choosing platforms. Whether it's brand awareness, lead generation, or community building, different platforms excel in different areas. Align your objectives with the strengths of the chosen platforms.

4. **Competitor Analysis:**

- Analyze the social media presence of your competitors. Identify which platforms they are most active on and assess their engagement levels. This analysis can provide valuable insights into where your target audience is already engaged.

5. **Resource and Time Constraints:**

- Consider the resources, both human and financial, available for managing social media. Each platform demands a unique approach and time commitment. Choose platforms that align with your capacity to consistently create and share content.

6. **Content-Type and Format:**

   - Evaluate the type of content your startup excels in creating. If your content is highly visual, platforms like Instagram or Pinterest may be more suitable. If your strength lies in industry insights and articles, LinkedIn or Twitter might be the preferred choice.

7. **Test and Iterate:**

   - Experiment with a few platforms initially and analyze the results. Use analytics tools to measure engagement, reach, and conversion rates. Based on the data, refine your strategy and focus on the platforms that yield the best results.

8. **Industry Relevance:**

   - Consider the industry your startup operates in. Certain industries may find better traction on specific platforms. Fashion and lifestyle brands often thrive on Instagram, while B2B startups might find success on LinkedIn.

9. **Emerging Platforms and Trends:**

   - Stay abreast of emerging platforms and social media trends. While established platforms provide stability, exploring newer ones can give your startup a competitive edge and help you reach untapped audiences.

10. **Integrated Marketing Strategy:**

    - Integrate your social media strategy with your overall marketing plan. Ensure coherence in messaging and branding across all platforms. A harmonized approach enhances brand recall and reinforces your startup's identity.

In conclusion, the process of choosing the right social media platforms for your startup is a strategic decision that requires a deep understanding of your audience, objectives, and resources. By aligning your choices with these considerations and remaining adaptable to changes in the digital landscape, your startup can build a strong and effective presence on social media.

- Setting SMART Goals for Social Media Success

Establishing clear and achievable goals is paramount for the success of your startup's social media strategy. SMART goals provide a framework that ensures your objectives are specific, measurable, attainable, relevant, and time-bound. In this comprehensive discussion, we delve into the importance of setting SMART goals for social media success and provide a step-by-step guide for their implementation.

1. **Specific (S):**

   - Clearly define the specifics of your social media goals. Instead of a vague objective like "increase engagement," specify the metric and context, such as "increase Instagram post engagement rate by 15% within the next quarter." Clarity helps in focusing efforts and measuring success accurately.

2. **Measurable (M):**

   - Establish metrics to quantifiably measure progress. Identify key performance indicators (KPIs) relevant to your goals, such as likes, shares, comments, or click-through rates. Measurable goals enable you to track performance and adjust strategies based on real data.

3. **Attainable (A):**

   - Ensure that your goals are realistically achievable. Consider the resources, team capabilities, and time constraints. Setting unattainable goals can lead to frustration and demotivation. Strike a balance between ambitious and feasible objectives to maintain momentum.

4. **Relevant (R):**

- Align your social media goals with your overall business objectives. Each goal should contribute directly to your startup's growth and success. Relevance ensures that your efforts on social media are in harmony with the broader strategic vision of your startup.

5. **Time-Bound (T):**

- Set a specific timeframe for achieving your goals. Whether it's weekly, monthly, or quarterly, a defined timeline creates a sense of urgency and facilitates effective planning. For instance, "Increase Facebook page likes by 20% in the next two months" provides a clear time boundary.

Implementing SMART Goals:

1. **Audit Current Performance:**

- Begin by assessing your startup's current social media performance. Identify strengths, weaknesses, and areas for improvement. This baseline assessment will inform the goals you set.

2. **Align with Business Objectives:**

- Ensure that your social media goals directly contribute to your startup's overarching business objectives. Whether it's increasing brand awareness, driving website traffic, or generating leads, alignment is crucial.

3. **Prioritize Key Metrics:**

- Select the most relevant KPIs for your goals. Whether it's follower growth, engagement rates, conversion rates, or reach, prioritize the metrics that best reflect the success of your social media efforts.

4. **Break Down Larger Goals:**

- If your overarching goal is substantial, break it down into smaller, more manageable objectives. This not only makes the process more achievable but also allows for incremental progress tracking.

5. **Regularly Review and Adjust:**

- Social media is dynamic, and your goals should be flexible. Regularly review your progress, analyze data, and be prepared to adjust your goals based on changing circumstances or emerging opportunities.

6. **Communicate Goals Across Teams:**

- Ensure that all relevant teams within your startup are aware of and aligned with the social media goals. Collaborate with marketing, sales, and other departments to foster a holistic approach to goal achievement.

7. **Celebrate Milestones:**

- Acknowledge and celebrate achievements along the way. Milestone celebrations not only boost morale but also serve as markers for reassessment and refinement of strategies for subsequent goals.

By adhering to the SMART criteria and implementing a structured approach, your startup can set social media goals that are not only ambitious but also strategic and attainable. This methodology empowers your team to navigate the dynamic landscape of social media with purpose, ensuring that every effort contributes meaningfully to the growth and success of your startup.

CHAPTER 2: CRAFTING COMPELLING CONTENT

In the digital realm, where attention is scarce and competition is fierce, the ability to craft compelling content stands as the linchpin of a successful social media strategy. "Crafting Compelling Content" is a chapter dedicated to unravelling the art and science behind creating content that not only captures the fleeting attention of your audience but also resonates deeply, leaving a lasting impact.

In this chapter, we embark on a journey to explore the fundamental principles and advanced techniques that transform ordinary content into a magnetic force in the vast landscape of social media. Whether you're navigating the visual allure of Instagram, the succinct messaging of Twitter, or the immersive world of video on platforms like TikTok, the principles discussed here are universally applicable.

From developing a strategic content strategy that aligns with your brand identity to mastering the intricacies of storytelling, visual aesthetics, and user-generated content, this chapter serves as a comprehensive guide. We delve into the psychology behind engaging content, understanding the nuances of your audience's preferences, and adapting your approach to suit the ever-evolving trends of the digital landscape.

So, whether you're a startup seeking to establish a formidable online presence or an established brand aiming to refresh your content strategy, "Crafting Compelling Content" equips you with the insights and practical tips needed to cut through the digital noise. Let's explore the power of words, images, and videos, and uncover the secrets to creating content that not only captures attention but fosters meaningful connections with your audience. Get ready to elevate your content game and make a lasting impression in the dynamic world of social media.

- Developing a Content Strategy Aligned with Your Brand

A well-crafted content strategy is the backbone of a successful social media presence, acting as a guiding force that aligns your brand identity with the expectations and preferences of your target audience. In this comprehensive discussion, we delve into the key components and strategies for developing a content strategy that resonates with your brand and fosters engagement and loyalty.

1. Understand Your Brand Identity:

- Begin by comprehensively understanding your brand identity. What values, personality traits, and unique aspects define your brand? This clarity serves as the foundation upon which your content strategy will be built.

2. Define Your Objectives:

- Clearly outline the objectives of your content strategy. Whether it's increasing brand awareness, driving website traffic, or promoting a new product, each piece of content should contribute to specific, measurable goals.

3. Know Your Audience:

- Conduct thorough audience research to understand the demographics, interests, and behaviors of your target audience. Tailor your content to resonate with their preferences, language, and aspirations, fostering a deeper connection.

4. Content Pillars and Themes:

- Identify core themes or content pillars that align with your brand values and resonate with your audience. These pillars act as consistent themes that tie your content together, creating a cohesive and recognizable brand presence.

5. Content Formats:

- Explore various content formats that suit your brand and engage your audience effectively. This may include blog posts, infographics, videos, podcasts, or a combination of these. Diversifying content formats keeps your strategy dynamic and caters to different audience preferences.

6. Consistency in Messaging:

- Maintain consistency in your brand messaging across all content. Whether it's the tone of voice, key messages, or visual elements, a uniform brand presence builds trust and reinforces your identity in the minds of your audience.

7. **Content Calendar and Scheduling:**

   - Develop a content calendar that outlines the frequency and timing of your posts. Consistent posting not only keeps your audience engaged but also contributes to algorithmic visibility on social media platforms.

8. **User-Generated Content (UGC):**

   - Encourage and leverage user-generated content. UGC adds authenticity to your brand, showcasing real experiences and interactions with your products or services. It also fosters a sense of community among your audience.

9. **Adaptability and Trend Integration:**

   - Stay agile in your approach by incorporating current trends and topics into your content strategy. This not only keeps your brand relevant but also demonstrates a responsiveness to the ever-evolving interests of your audience.

10. Data Analysis and Iteration:

   - Regularly analyze the performance of your content using analytics tools. Assess metrics such as engagement rates, reach, and conversion. Use the insights gained to refine and optimize your content strategy over time.

11. Brand Storytelling:

   - Weave your brand story into your content. Whether it's the narrative of your founding, customer success stories, or behind-the-scenes glimpses, storytelling adds depth and emotional connection to your brand.

12. Engagement and Community Building:

- Foster engagement by responding to comments, messages, and interactions promptly. Actively participate in conversations and build a sense of community around your brand. Engagement is a two-way street that strengthens relationships.

In conclusion, a content strategy aligned with your brand is a dynamic and adaptive roadmap that navigates the digital landscape with purpose. By consistently delivering valuable, authentic, and engaging content, your startup can forge a strong and enduring connection with its audience, laying the groundwork for sustained social media success.

- Mastering Visual Content: Graphics, Images, and Videos

In the visually-driven landscape of social media, mastering the art of visual content is a nonnegotiable component for capturing attention, conveying brand identity, and fostering engagement. This comprehensive discussion explores the significance of graphics, images, and videos in your content strategy and provides insights on how to create compelling visual content that aligns with your brand.

1. **Importance of Visual Content:**

   - Visuals are processed faster by the human brain than text. They evoke emotions, enhance storytelling, and contribute to better message retention. Visual content is pivotal for creating a memorable and impactful brand presence on social media.

2. **Consistent Brand Aesthetics:**

   - Establish a consistent visual aesthetic that aligns with your brand identity. From color schemes and typography to design elements, consistency across all visual content reinforces brand recognition and strengthens the overall brand image.

3. **Professional Graphics Design**:

  - Invest in professional graphic design for your visual content. High-quality graphics elevate the perceived value of your brand and contribute to a polished and professional appearance. Tools like Adobe Creative Suite or Canva can aid in creating visually appealing designs.

4. **Compelling Images:**

  - Curate and create high-quality images that resonate with your brand narrative. Authentic, original visuals perform well on social media, as they convey sincerity and transparency. Professional photography or well-curated stock images can enhance your visual storytelling.

5. **Engaging Videos:**

- Videos are a powerful medium for storytelling. Create engaging and shareable videos that align with your brand. This could include product demonstrations, behind-the-scenes footage, customer testimonials, or educational content. Leverage platforms like YouTube, Instagram, and TikTok for diverse video content.

6. **Infographics for Informational Content:**

   - Infographics are effective for conveying complex information in a visually appealing and easily digestible format. Use infographics to share statistics, data, or step-by-step guides. Tools like Piktochart or Canva make infographic creation accessible.

7. **Custom Branded Templates:**

   - Develop custom-branded templates for consistency in visual content creation. Whether it's for social media posts, stories, or promotional material, templates provide a framework that maintains visual coherence across various platforms.

8. **Visual Storytelling:**

- Infuse your visual content with storytelling elements. Craft narratives that resonate emotionally, and use visuals to complement and enhance the narrative. A well-told story through visuals can create a lasting impact on your audience.

9. **Accessibility Considerations:**

- Ensure your visual content is accessible to a diverse audience. Incorporate alt text for images, use readable fonts, and consider color contrast for better accessibility. Accessibility not only broadens your audience but also reflects a commitment to inclusivity.

10. **Responsive Design for Mobile:**

- Optimize visual content for mobile viewing. With the majority of social media users accessing platforms on mobile devices, ensuring that your visuals are mobile-friendly is crucial for a seamless and enjoyable user experience.

11. **User-Generated Visual Content:**

   - Encourage and showcase user-generated visual content. This not only adds authenticity but also turns your audience into brand advocates. Implement branded hashtags to gather and showcase user-generated visuals.

12. **Analytics and Iteration:**

   - Utilize analytics to assess the performance of your visual content. Track metrics such as engagement, reach, and conversion rates. Based on the data, refine and iterate your visual content strategy to align with audience preferences.

In conclusion, mastering visual content is an essential aspect of a robust social media strategy. By prioritizing high-quality, consistent, and engaging visuals, your startup can not only capture the attention of your audience but also convey a compelling brand narrative that resonates on a visual and emotional level.

- The Power of Storytelling in Captivating Your Audience

Storytelling is a timeless and powerful tool that transcends cultures, connects individuals, and can captivate an audience on a profound level. In the dynamic landscape of social media, where attention spans are fleeting, the art of storytelling becomes a cornerstone for building meaningful connections with your audience. This comprehensive discussion explores the significance of storytelling and provides insights into how it can be harnessed to engage and captivate your social media audience.

1. **Emotional Resonance:**

   - Storytelling taps into the emotional core of your audience. By weaving narratives that evoke emotions such as joy, empathy, or inspiration, you create a memorable and relatable experience that resonates deeply with your audience.

2. **Humanizing Your Brand:**

   - Stories humanize your brand by offering a glimpse into the people, values, and experiences that shape it. Sharing the human side of your startup fosters authenticity, making your brand more approachable and relatable to your audience.

3. **Building a Narrative Arc:**

   - Craft narratives with a clear arc that includes an introduction, rising action, climax, falling action, and resolution. A well-structured story keeps your audience engaged, building anticipation and emotional connection throughout the narrative.

4. Aligning with Brand Values:

- Your brand story should align with your core values. Whether it's sustainability, innovation, or social responsibility, integrating these values into your narrative reinforces your brand identity and attracts like-minded individuals.

5. Relatable Characters and Scenarios:

- Create relatable characters and scenarios within your stories. Your audience should see themselves in the narrative, fostering a sense of connection and understanding. Realistic and relatable stories resonate more profoundly.

6. Visual Storytelling:

- Combine visual elements with your storytelling. Use images, graphics, and videos to enhance the narrative. Visual storytelling not only captures attention but also conveys messages in a more immersive and memorable way.

7. **Consistency Across Platforms:**

   - Maintain consistency in your brand storytelling across all social media platforms. Whether it's a short anecdote on Twitter, a longer-form narrative on LinkedIn, or a visual story on Instagram, coherence reinforces brand identity.

8. **Interactive Storytelling**:

   - Foster interactivity by involving your audience in your stories. Ask questions, prompt responses, or encourage user-generated content related to your narrative. Interactive storytelling transforms passive viewers into active participants.

9. **Brand Origin and Milestones:**

- Share the origin story of your startup and key milestones in your journey. These narratives not only provide context but also showcase the growth and evolution of your brand, building a sense of continuity and progress.

10. **Educational Storytelling:**

- Use storytelling as a vehicle for education. Whether it's explaining complex concepts, sharing industry insights, or providing tutorials, educational storytelling positions your brand as an authority in your field while adding value to your audience.

11. **Story Series and Continuity:**

- Develop story series or recurring themes that create continuity. Serialized storytelling keeps your audience coming back for more, anticipating the next chapter or instalment in your narrative.

12. Authenticity and Transparency:

- Be authentic and transparent in your storytelling. Audiences appreciate genuine narratives that showcase both successes and challenges. Authenticity builds trust and strengthens the connection between your brand and your audience.

In conclusion, the power of storytelling in captivating your social media audience lies in its ability to create emotional connections, convey values, and make your brand memorable. By leveraging the art of storytelling across your social media platforms, your startup can transform casual observers into engaged and loyal followers, fostering a community that resonates with the narrative you craft.

- Utilizing User-Generated Content for Authenticity

User-generated content (UGC) has emerged as a potent tool for establishing authenticity, building trust, and fostering community engagement in the realm of social media. By empowering your audience to contribute content, you not only diversify your content strategy but also create a genuine and relatable brand image. In this comprehensive discussion, we explore the significance of user-generated content and provide insights on how to effectively leverage it for authenticity on social media.

1. **Defining User-Generated Content (UGC):**

   - User-generated content refers to any content created by your audience rather than your brand.

This can include photos, videos, testimonials, reviews, and social media posts that feature your products or services.

2. **Authenticity and Trust:**

   - UGC is inherently authentic as it reflects the real experiences and perspectives of your audience. By showcasing content created by actual users, you build trust and credibility, as potential customers are more likely to trust the opinions of their peers.

3. **Encouraging Participation:**

   - Actively encourage your audience to contribute content. This can be done through branded hashtags, contests, challenges, or simply by prompting users to share their experiences. Creating a culture of participation enhances community engagement.

4. **Showcasing Diversity:**

- UGC allows you to showcase the diversity of your audience. Different individuals, lifestyles, and experiences are represented in the content, creating a more inclusive and relatable brand image that resonates with a broader audience.

5. **Curating and Showcasing UGC:**

- Curate and showcase the best UGC on your social media platforms. This not only provides valuable social proof but also gives credit to your audience, encouraging further participation. Acknowledging and thanking contributors strengthens the sense of community.

6. **Consent and Permissions:**

- Obtain consent and permissions before using UGC. Ensure that you have the right to share and showcase the content. This not only respects the privacy of your audience but also establishes a transparent and ethical approach to UGC utilization.

7. Interactive Campaigns:

- Design interactive campaigns that prompt users to create and share content. Whether it's a challenge, a storytelling campaign, or a creative contest, interactive campaigns stimulate engagement and generate a stream of diverse UGCs.

8. Monitoring and Moderation:

- Implement a system for monitoring and moderating UGC. This ensures that the content aligns with your brand values and guidelines. Proactive moderation maintains a positive and brand-aligned environment.

9. Integrating UGC into Marketing Strategies:

- Integrate UGC into your broader marketing strategies. Utilize UGC in advertising, email campaigns, and website content. Integrating user-generated visuals and testimonials across channels reinforces authenticity and social proof.

10. **Highlighting Customer Stories:**

   - Showcase in-depth customer stories that go beyond a single post. Feature testimonials, success stories, or day-in-the-life narratives. Humanizing your customers in this way adds depth and personalization to your brand.

11. **Leveraging Instagram Stories and Reels:**

   - Utilize Instagram Stories and Reels to feature UGC in a dynamic and ephemeral format. This adds a sense of urgency and exclusivity to the content, encouraging more users to participate.

12. **Listening and Responding:**

   - Actively listen to your audience and respond to their UGC. Engage in conversations, express gratitude, and build a dialogue. The responsiveness enhances the sense of community and encourages ongoing contributions.

In conclusion, user-generated content serves as a powerful vehicle for authenticity on social media. By actively involving your audience in the content creation process, you not only build trust but also create a dynamic and diverse representation of your brand. Through strategic encouragement, curation, and integration, UGC becomes a cornerstone in crafting an authentic and relatable brand image in the digital landscape.

CHAPTER 3: OPTIMIZING YOUR SOCIAL MEDIA PROFILES

In the vast and bustling world of social media, your profile is the digital storefront of your brand, the first impression that sets the tone for your audience's engagement. "Optimizing Your Social Media Profiles" is a chapter dedicated to navigating the intricacies of crafting profiles that not only reflect your brand identity but also maximize visibility and engagement.

In this chapter, we embark on a journey to unravel the art of optimization — from refining your profile bio to selecting the perfect visual elements. Every pixel and character contributes to the narrative of your brand, and every strategic choice enhances your discoverability on these dynamic platforms.

As we delve into the nuances of social media optimization, we'll explore the importance of crafting an irresistible profile bio, designing eye-catching visuals, leveraging platform features for maximum visibility, and maintaining consistency across all your online outposts. Join me as we unravel the secrets to creating profiles that not only stand out in the crowded digital landscape but also invite your audience to connect, engage, and become an integral part of your brand's journey. Let's optimize together, ensuring that your social media profiles serve as compelling gateways to the rich tapestry of your brand's story.

- Crafting an Irresistible Profile Bio

In the realm of social media, where attention spans are short and first impressions are crucial, your profile bio acts as the digital handshake that introduces your brand to the world. Crafting an irresistible profile bio is an art that involves conciseness, clarity, and creativity. In this comprehensive discussion, we delve into the key elements and strategies for creating a profile bio that captivates your audience and communicates the essence of your brand.

1. **Clarity and Conciseness:**

   - Start with clarity and conciseness. Your bio should succinctly communicate who you are, what you do, and why it matters. Avoid jargon and prioritize straightforward language that is easily understood by a diverse audience.

2. Value Proposition:

- Clearly articulate your value proposition. What sets your brand apart? Whether it's unique products, exceptional services, or a distinctive mission, highlight the elements that make your brand irresistible to your target audience.

3. Keyword Optimization:

- Incorporate relevant keywords that align with your brand and industry. This not only improves the discoverability of your profile but also enhances its search engine optimization (SEO) on the platform.

4. Humanizing Elements:

- Infuse humanizing elements into your bio. Share the personality of your brand, whether it's through humor, authenticity, or relatability. Humanized bios resonate more deeply with audiences, forging a connection beyond the transactional.

5. Call-to-Action (CTA):

- Include a clear and compelling call to action. Whether it's directing users to your website, inviting them to explore your latest products, or encouraging them to share their experiences with a branded hashtag, guide your audience on the next steps.

6. **Emojis and Symbols:**

- Emojis and symbols can add visual appeal and personality to your bio. Use them strategically to break up text, highlight key points, or convey emotions. However, exercise moderation to maintain a professional appearance.

7. **Contact Information:**

- If relevant, include contact information such as an email address or a link to your website. Make it easy for potential customers, collaborators, or media to connect with you beyond the social media platform.

8. **Hashtags and Mentions:**

- Incorporate relevant hashtags and mentions in your bio. This not only connects your brand with broader conversations but also increases the likelihood of being discovered by users interested in those topics.

9. **Achievements and Accolades**:

   - Showcase notable achievements, accolades, or affiliations. This builds credibility and trust with your audience, demonstrating your brand's expertise and recognition in the industry.

10. **Updates and Freshness:**

   - Regularly update your bio to reflect changes in your brand, promotions, or any recent accomplishments. Keeping your bio current ensures that your audience receives the most accurate and relevant information.

11. **Brand Voice and Tone:**

- Align your bio with the overall voice and tone of your brand. Whether it's formal, casual, friendly, or professional, maintaining consistency across all brand communication channels reinforces brand identity.

12. **Review and Refinement:**

- Periodically review and refine your bio based on feedback, changes in your business, or evolving brand positioning. An optimized bio is a dynamic and evolving element of your social media strategy.

In conclusion, crafting an irresistible profile bio is a strategic endeavor that requires a deep understanding of your brand identity and a keen awareness of your target audience. By distilling the essence of your brand into a concise, engaging, and impactful bio, you set the stage for meaningful connections, increased visibility, and a positive first impression in the digital landscape.

- Designing Eye-Catching Visuals for Profile Elements

In the visually-driven world of social media, first impressions often rely on the visual appeal of your profile elements. From profile pictures to cover images, and even the overall aesthetics of your posts, designing eye-catching visuals is paramount for capturing attention and communicating the essence of your brand. In this comprehensive discussion, we explore the key principles and strategies for creating visually stunning profile elements that leave a lasting impact on your audience.

1. **Consistent Branding:**

   - Begin with a consistent visual identity. Use the same color palette, fonts, and design elements across all your profile visuals. Consistent branding reinforces recognition and establishes a cohesive visual presence.

2. **High-Quality Imagery:**

- Prioritize high-quality images for your profile picture, cover photo, and any other visual elements. Clear, sharp, and well-composed images enhance the professionalism and visual appeal of your profile.

3. **Profile Picture:**

- Your profile picture is often the first visual element users see. Choose a clear and recognizable image that reflects your brand identity. Whether it's a logo, a headshot, or a product image, ensure it is easily identifiable, even in a small format.

4. **Cover Photo:**

- Utilize the cover photo to convey additional information about your brand or showcase key products or services. Ensure that the cover photo complements the profile picture and aligns with your overall brand aesthetics.

5. **Graphics and Illustrations:**

   - Incorporate custom graphics or illustrations that align with your brand personality. These can be used to highlight key messages, create visual interest in posts, or add a unique touch to your profile.

6. **Text Overlay:**

   - When using images, consider adding text overlay to convey messages or share key information. Use readable fonts, contrasting colors, and concise language to ensure that the text is easily digestible.

7. **Visual Hierarchy:**

   - Establish a visual hierarchy in your profile visuals. Guide the viewer's attention by prioritizing key elements. This could be achieved through size, color, or positioning, ensuring that the most important information stands out.

8. **Platform-Specific Dimensions:**

   - Be mindful of platform-specific dimensions for profile pictures and cover photos. Each social media platform has its own recommended sizes, and optimizing visuals for these dimensions ensures a polished and professional appearance.

9. **Story Highlights and Icons:**

   - If applicable, design custom icons for your story highlights on platforms like Instagram. These icons can visually represent different categories or aspects of your brand, adding a personalized touch to your profile.

10. **Visual Content Templates:**

    - Create visual content templates for consistency in your posts. Whether it's quote graphics, promotional images, or announcements, having predefined templates streamlines the content creation process while maintaining a cohesive visual identity.

11. **White Space and Simplicity:**

   - Embrace white space and simplicity in your visuals. Cluttered visuals can be overwhelming, while clean and well-balanced designs contribute to a more aesthetically pleasing and user-friendly profile.

12. **Accessibility Considerations:**

   - Ensure that your visuals are accessible to all users, including those with disabilities. Use high contrast for text, provide alternative text for images, and follow accessibility guidelines to create an inclusive visual experience.

13. **Adaptability across Devices:**

- Test the adaptability of your visuals across various devices. Given the diverse ways users access social media, from desktops to smartphones and tablets, visuals should be optimized for a seamless experience on different screen sizes.

In conclusion, designing eye-catching visuals for profile elements is an integral aspect of a compelling social media strategy. By adhering to principles of consistency, quality, and user-friendly design, your brand can create a visually captivating presence that not only captures attention but also communicates the essence of your brand to a diverse and discerning audience.

- Leveraging Features and Settings for Maximum Visibility

Optimizing the features and settings of your social media profiles is a strategic endeavor that can significantly enhance your brand's visibility and engagement. From utilizing algorithm-friendly content to harnessing platform-specific features, this comprehensive discussion explores the key strategies for leveraging features and settings to ensure maximum visibility across various social media platforms.

1. **Algorithm-Friendly Content:**

   - Understand the algorithms of each platform and tailor your content accordingly. Platforms like Instagram, Facebook, and Twitter prioritize different factors in their algorithms, such as engagement, relevancy, and recency. Craft content that aligns with these algorithms to enhance visibility.

2. **Hashtags and Keywords:**

   - Harness the power of hashtags and keywords to expand the reach of your content. Research and use relevant and trending hashtags on platforms like Instagram and Twitter. Incorporate keywords strategically in your captions, bio, and posts for improved discoverability.

3. **Geotagging:**

   - Utilize geotagging features to connect with local audiences. Whether you're a local business or hosting events, geotagging enhances the visibility of your content to users in specific locations.

4. **Platform-Specific Features:**

   - Leverage unique features offered by each platform. Instagram offers Stories, Reels, and

IGTV, while LinkedIn has LinkedIn Live and document sharing. Exploring and incorporating platform-specific features diversifies your content and engages users in different ways.

5. **Profile Completion:**

 - Ensure that your profile is complete with all relevant information. This includes a comprehensive bio, contact details, website links, and any other fields provided by the platform. A complete profile not only builds credibility but also enhances visibility in searches.

6. **Engagement with Followers:**

 - Actively engage with your followers through likes, comments, and direct messages. Platforms often prioritize content from accounts that engage with their audience. Genuine interactions not only boost visibility but also foster a sense of community.

7. Consistent Posting Schedule:

- Establish a consistent posting schedule. Regular and predictable posting signals to algorithms that your content is active and relevant. Consistency contributes to better visibility and engagement.

8. Ad Campaigns and Promotions:

- Utilize paid advertising features on platforms to amplify your reach. Social media platforms offer targeted ad campaigns that allow you to reach specific demographics. Invest strategically in paid promotions for maximum visibility.

9. Content Distribution Timing:

- Pay attention to the timing of your content distribution. Analyze when your audience is most active and schedule your posts during those peak times. Timely distribution ensures that your content is more likely to appear in users' feeds.

10. Community Engagement Groups:

- Join or create community engagement groups where users support each other by liking, commenting, and sharing content. These groups can boost the initial engagement of your posts, signaling algorithms to promote them further.

11. **Visibility Settings and Privacy:**

- Review your privacy settings to ensure that your content is visible to the desired audience. Understand the implications of public versus private profiles, and adjust settings accordingly to strike a balance between visibility and privacy.

12. **Analytics and Insights:**

- Regularly monitor analytics and insights provided by the platforms. Understand what types of content perform well, identify trends, and adjust your strategy based on data-driven insights. Analytics provide valuable information for refining your approach.

13. Cross-Promotion:

- Cross-promote your content across different platforms. Share snippets or highlights on one platform that lead users to your presence on another. Cross-promotion expands your audience reach and encourages followers to engage across multiple channels.

In conclusion, leveraging features and settings for maximum visibility requires a strategic and holistic approach. By aligning with platform algorithms, utilizing unique features, and optimizing your profile settings, your brand can increase its visibility, engage a broader audience, and foster a vibrant and active online community.

- Maintaining Consistency Across Platforms

Consistency in your online presence is a powerful strategy for building a strong and recognizable brand. It involves presenting a unified image and message across various social media platforms to create a cohesive and memorable brand identity. In this comprehensive discussion, we explore the key principles and strategies for maintaining consistency across different social media platforms.

1. **Unified Branding Elements:**

   - Start by establishing unified branding elements, including your logo, color scheme, typography, and any visual elements that represent your brand. Consistency in these elements creates a cohesive visual identity across platforms.

2. Consistent Profile Information:

   - Ensure that your profile information, such as bio, contact details, and website links, is consistent across all platforms. Unified and accurate information builds credibility and helps users easily identify your brand.

3. Profile Imagery:

   - Use consistent profile imagery, including profile pictures and cover photos, across all platforms. This visual consistency reinforces brand recognition and ensures that users can easily associate your profiles with your brand.

4. Content Style and Tone:

   - Maintain a consistent style and tone in your content. Whether it's the language you use, the type of imagery, or the overall vibe, coherence in content style establishes a distinct and recognizable brand voice.

5. **Posting Schedule:**

   - Establish a consistent posting schedule. While the frequency of posts may vary based on platform dynamics, maintaining a regular schedule ensures that your audience anticipates and engages with your content regularly.

6. **Adaptation to Platform Nuances:**

   - While consistency is crucial, it's also important to adapt to the nuances of each platform. Tailor your content to fit the format and audience expectations of each platform, ensuring that your message remains consistent while optimizing for the platform's strengths.

7. **Cross-Platform Campaigns:**

   - Implement cross-platform campaigns that maintain a central theme or message while utilizing the unique features of each platform. This approach ensures consistency in messaging while catering to the preferences of diverse audiences.

8. Uniform Messaging:

- Ensure that your key messages and value propositions are consistent across all platforms. Unified messaging helps reinforce brand identity and ensures that users receive a cohesive narrative regardless of the platform they engage with.

9. Color and Design Consistency:

- Maintain consistency in color schemes, design elements, and visual aesthetics. This extends to graphics, images, and any other visual content. Consistent visuals contribute to a harmonious and easily recognizable brand image.

10. Responsive Customer Engagement:

- Consistency in customer engagement is crucial. Respond to comments, messages, and interactions promptly and consistently across all platforms. Uniformly engaging with your audience strengthens relationships and fosters trust.

11. **Coordinated Campaigns:**

   - Coordinate marketing campaigns across platforms to create a synchronized brand experience. Whether it's a product launch, promotion, or event, a cohesive and coordinated approach enhances the impact of your campaigns.

12. **Monitoring and Feedback Loop:**

   - Continuously monitor your brand's performance and collect feedback from your audience. Use analytics tools to assess the success of your consistency efforts and make adjustments based on insights and evolving trends.

13. Employee Advocacy Guidelines:

- If applicable, provide guidelines for employee advocacy to maintain consistency in the way employees represent the brand on their personal social media accounts. This ensures a unified external perception of the brand.

In conclusion, maintaining consistency across platforms is a dynamic and strategic effort that requires a careful balance between uniformity and adaptability. By aligning visual elements, messaging, and engagement practices, your brand can create a seamless and recognizable experience for your audience, reinforcing trust, loyalty, and a strong brand presence across the diverse landscape of social media.

CHAPTER 4: STRATEGIC ENGAGEMENT AND COMMUNITY BUILDING

In the dynamic realm of social media, the true essence of a brand's success lies not just in the number of followers, but in the depth of engagement and the sense of community it fosters. "Strategic Engagement and Community Building" is a chapter dedicated to unravelling the intricacies of cultivating meaningful connections in the digital space.

Beyond mere likes and shares, this chapter delves into the art and strategy of engaging with your audience strategically. From responding to comments and messages to initiating conversations and creating a sense of community, every interaction contributes to the narrative of your brand.

As we explore the depths of strategic engagement, we will unravel techniques for fostering a sense of belonging, encouraging user-generated content, and building a vibrant online community. Join me on this journey as we discover the strategic nuances that transform casual observers into engaged followers and cultivate a community that resonates with the values and aspirations of your brand. Let's delve into the world of strategic engagement and community building, where every interaction becomes a building block in the architecture of a thriving digital community.

- Building and Nurturing an Engaged Community

In the dynamic landscape of social media, building and nurturing an engaged community is a cornerstone for the long-term success of any brand. An engaged community not only forms the backbone of brand loyalty but also serves as a dynamic space for meaningful interactions, user-generated content, and invaluable feedback. This comprehensive discussion explores the strategies and principles behind building and nurturing a thriving community on social media platforms.

1. **Define Your Community Purpose:**

   - Clearly define the purpose and goals of your community. Whether it's providing support, sharing expertise, or fostering a shared passion, a well-defined purpose attracts like-minded individuals and sets the foundation for community building.

2. **Authenticity and Transparency:**

   - Cultivate authenticity and transparency in your interactions. Share behind-the-scenes glimpses, acknowledge challenges, and celebrate successes. Authenticity builds trust and resonates with community members on a personal level.

3. **Active Listening:**

   - Actively listen to your community members. Monitor comments, messages, and social media mentions to understand their needs, concerns, and feedback. Engaging in active listening fosters a sense of being heard and valued.

4. **Consistent Communication:**

   - Establish a consistent communication strategy. Regularly update your community on relevant information, news, and events. Consistency in communication maintains engagement and keeps the community informed.

5. **Encourage User-Generated Content (UGC):**

- Actively encourage and celebrate user-generated content. Whether it's testimonials, photos, or creative expressions, UGC not only showcases the diversity within the community but also serves as a powerful form of social proof.

6. **Initiate Conversations:**

- Take the lead in initiating conversations. Pose questions, start polls, or create discussions around relevant topics. Initiating conversations not only sparks engagement but also positions your brand as a facilitator of meaningful interactions.

7. **Community Guidelines:**

- Establish clear community guidelines. Communicate the values, expectations, and rules within the community. Well-defined guidelines create a positive and respectful environment that encourages open dialogue.

8. **Recognition and Appreciation:**

- Recognize and appreciate community members. Highlight their contributions, celebrate milestones, and express gratitude. Recognition fosters a sense of belonging and motivates members to actively participate.

9. **Exclusive Content and Offers:**

- Provide exclusive content, sneak peeks, or special offers to community members. Creating a sense of exclusivity adds value to community participation and incentivizes members to remain engaged.

10. Moderation and Conflict Resolution:

   - Implement effective moderation to maintain a positive atmosphere. Address conflicts promptly and diplomatically. A well-moderated community ensures a safe and welcoming space for all members.

11. Collaborations and Partnerships:

   - Explore collaborations and partnerships within the community. Whether it's featuring member stories or collaborating on projects, fostering a collaborative environment strengthens the bonds within the community.

12. Interactive Events:

- Organize interactive events such as webinars, live Q&A sessions, or virtual meetups. Interactive events provide opportunities for real-time engagement and strengthen the sense of community connection.

13. Feedback Loops:

- Establish feedback loops to gather insights from the community. Seek feedback on products, services, or community initiatives. Incorporate community suggestions and demonstrate a commitment to continuous improvement.

14. Evolve with the Community:

- Be flexible and adaptive to the evolving needs of the community. As the community grows, be open to incorporating new features, adjusting strategies, and evolving to meet the changing dynamics of your audience.

15. Community Metrics and Analysis:

- Utilize analytics tools to measure community metrics. Track engagement rates, growth, and sentiment. Analyzing data provides valuable insights for refining community strategies and identifying areas for improvement.

In conclusion, building and nurturing an engaged community is a multifaceted endeavor that requires a blend of authenticity, active engagement, and a commitment to community values. By fostering a space where members feel heard, valued, and connected, brands can cultivate a vibrant community that not only supports their goals but also thrives as a dynamic and collaborative digital ecosystem.

- Effective Use of Hashtags and Trend Participation

In the ever-evolving landscape of social media, hashtags have become a ubiquitous tool for content discovery and trend participation. Mastering the effective use of hashtags is a strategic imperative for brands seeking to enhance visibility, engage with a broader audience, and stay relevant in dynamic online conversations. This comprehensive discussion explores the principles and strategies behind the effective use of hashtags and trend participation.

1. **Understand Platform-Specific Dynamics:**

   - Different social media platforms have distinct dynamics when it comes to hashtags. Platforms like Instagram and Twitter heavily rely on hashtags for content discovery, while others, like LinkedIn, prioritize a more curated use. Understand the nuances of each platform to tailor your hashtag strategy accordingly.

2. **Research and Select Relevant Hashtags:**

   - Conduct thorough research to identify relevant and popular hashtags within your industry or niche. Consider both broad and niche-specific hashtags to maximize reach while targeting a more engaged audience interested in your content.

3. **Create Branded Hashtags:**

   - Develop and promote branded hashtags specific to your brand or campaigns. Branded hashtags not only encourage user-generated content but also contribute to building a unique brand identity. Ensure that your branded hashtags are memorable, easy to spell, and reflective of your brand's personality.

4. **Diversify Hashtag Usage:**

   - Mix popular and niche hashtags in your content. While popular hashtags can expose your content to a broader audience, niche hashtags help target a more specific and engaged community. A balanced approach ensures visibility and relevance.

5. **Monitor Trending Hashtags:**

   - Stay attuned to trending hashtags within your industry or on a broader scale. Participating in relevant trends can amplify your content's visibility and connect your brand with ongoing conversations. However, ensure alignment with your brand values to maintain authenticity.

6. **Tailor Hashtags to Campaigns and Content:**

   - Customize your hashtags to align with specific campaigns, promotions, or content themes. Tailoring hashtags ensures cohesiveness in messaging and allows your audience to associate specific hashtags with distinct aspects of your brand.

7. **Limit and Position Hashtags Strategically:**

   - While Instagram allows for a higher number of hashtags, other platforms like Twitter may benefit from a more conservative approach. Position your hashtags strategically within your caption or comments to maintain a clean and readable aesthetic while still maximizing visibility.

8. **Encourage User Participation:**

   - Actively encourage your audience to use your branded hashtags and participate in relevant trends. User-generated content not only boosts engagement but also extends your brand's reach as followers share their content using your hashtags.

9. **Create and Engage in Hashtag Challenges:**

   - Initiate hashtag challenges to foster community engagement. Challenges encourage followers to create content based on a specific theme or prompt, contributing to a sense of community and virality around your brand.

10. **Utilize Hashtags in Stories and Reels:**

   - Incorporate hashtags in your Stories and Reels. While Instagram Stories allow for more interactive and dynamic use of hashtags, platforms like TikTok thrive on hashtag utilization. Leverage these features for increased discoverability.

11. **Monitor Analytics and Performance:**

   - Regularly monitor the performance of your hashtags using platform analytics. Analyzing reach, impressions, and engagement associated with specific hashtags provides valuable insights into the effectiveness of your hashtag strategy.

12. **Stay Contextually Relevant:**

   - Maintain contextually relevant hashtag usage. Ensure that the hashtags you incorporate align with the content of your post. Contextual relevance enhances the authenticity of your engagement and avoids the appearance of spam.

13. **Participate in Industry-Specific Chats:**

   - Engage in industry-specific Twitter chats or other themed conversations. Participating in relevant discussions using designated hashtags positions your brand as an active and informed participant within your industry.

14. **Create Evergreen Hashtags:**

   - Establish evergreen hashtags that can be consistently used across various campaigns and content. Evergreen hashtags contribute to long-term brand recognition and can serve as a unifying thread in your social media presence.

15. **Adjust and Experiment:**

   - Social media trends and algorithms evolve. Be willing to adjust your hashtag strategy and experiment with new trends or approaches. Flexibility and a willingness to adapt ensure that your brand remains dynamic and responsive in the digital landscape.

In conclusion, the effective use of hashtags and trend participation is an art that requires a nuanced understanding of platform dynamics, audience preferences, and industry trends. By crafting a strategic and well-researched hashtag strategy, brands can not only enhance their visibility but also actively participate in the vibrant and ever-changing conversations that define the social media landscape.

- Creating Contests and Giveaways to Boost Engagement

Contests and giveaways are powerful tools in a brand's social media arsenal, providing a dynamic way to boost engagement, expand reach, and foster a sense of excitement among the audience. This comprehensive discussion explores the strategies and best practices for creating effective contests and giveaways that captivate your audience and elevate your brand presence on social media.

1. **Set Clear Objectives:**

   - Begin by defining clear objectives for your contest or giveaway. Whether it's increasing brand awareness, growing your social media following, or promoting a new product, having well-defined goals helps shape the structure and mechanics of your campaign.

2. **Select the Right Platform:**

- Choose the social media platform that aligns with your target audience and campaign goals. Each platform has its dynamics, and selecting the right one ensures optimal engagement and participation.

3. **Understand Your Audience:**

- Tailor your contest or giveaway to match the preferences and behaviors of your target audience. Consider their interests, demographics, and preferred interaction styles to create a campaign that resonates with them.

4. **Craft Compelling Prizes:**

- Design prizes that are enticing and relevant to your audience. The value of the prizes should align with the effort required for participation. Prizes can include your products, exclusive experiences, or collaborations with other brands.

5. **Establish Clear Entry Guidelines:**

   - Clearly outline entry guidelines to eliminate confusion and encourage participation. Specify how participants can enter, what actions are required, and any additional steps, such as tagging friends or sharing the contest post.

6. **Utilize User-Generated Content (UGC):**

   - Encourage participants to create and share user-generated content as part of the contest. This not only increases engagement but also generates authentic content that showcases your brand in the context of your audience's experiences.

7. **Create a Branded Hashtag:**

   - Introduce a branded hashtag for your contest or giveaway. This hashtag not only helps in tracking entries but also facilitates user-generated content curation. Encourage participants to use the hashtag in their submissions.

8. **Leverage Entry Mechanisms:**

   - Provide multiple entry mechanisms to cater to different preferences. This can include likes, comments, shares, or more creative actions like photo submissions or answering questions. Diversifying entry mechanisms accommodates various user preferences.

9. **Establish a Timeline:**

   - Define a clear timeline for your contest or giveaway, including start and end dates. Creating a sense of urgency motivates participants to act promptly and ensures that your campaign maintains momentum.

10. Promote Across Channels:

- Promote your contest or giveaway across all your marketing channels. Leverage email newsletters, website banners, and other social media platforms to maximize reach and participation. Consistent cross-channel promotion amplifies the campaign's impact.

11. Engage with Participants:

- Actively engage with participants throughout the contest. Respond to comments, express gratitude for entries, and maintain an interactive presence. Engaging with participants enhances the overall experience and builds a positive brand perception.

12. Encourage Virality:

- Build virality into your campaign by incorporating elements that encourage participants to share with their networks. This can include bonus entries for referrals, challenges that require tagging friends, or sharing user-generated content.

13. **Comply with Platform Rules:**

- Familiarize yourself with and adhere to the rules and guidelines of the social media platforms hosting your contest. Each platform may have specific regulations regarding contests, giveaways, and promotional activities.

14. **Announce Winners Transparently:**

- When the contest concludes, announce the winners transparently. Use a live video, a dedicated post, or a story to publicly congratulate the winners. Transparency in announcing winners builds trust and maintains the integrity of your brand.

15. **Follow Up and Thank Participants:**

- After the contest or giveaway, follow up with a thank-you message to participants. Express gratitude for their engagement and communicate any future promotions or events. This post-contest communication helps retain the positive momentum generated by the campaign.

16. **Analyze Metrics and Learn:**

   - Analyze the performance metrics of your content, including engagement, reach, and new followers. Use these insights to understand what worked well and areas for improvement. Apply these learnings to enhance the success of future contests and giveaways.

In conclusion, creating contests and giveaways is a dynamic strategy for boosting engagement and creating excitement around your brand on social media. By aligning with your audience's preferences, offering compelling prizes, and fostering an interactive and transparent experience, your brand can not only achieve short-term engagement goals but also build lasting connections with your audience.

- Leveraging Social Listening for Customer Insights

Social listening is a dynamic approach that goes beyond monitoring brand mentions; it involves actively analyzing and interpreting social media conversations to gain valuable customer insights. By tapping into the vast pool of online discussions, brands can uncover trends, understand sentiment, and refine strategies based on real-time feedback. This comprehensive discussion explores the strategies and benefits of leveraging social listening for profound customer insights.

1. Define Objectives and Key Metrics:

- Begin by clearly defining your objectives for social listening. Whether it's understanding customer sentiment, tracking industry trends, or monitoring brand perception, establish key metrics to measure the success of your social listening efforts.

2. **Select Appropriate Social Listening Tools:**

- Choose robust social listening tools that align with your goals and scale. Platforms like Brandwatch, Hootsuite, and Mention provide features for tracking brand mentions, sentiment analysis, and monitoring relevant keywords across various social media channels.

3. **Identify Relevant Keywords and Topics:**

- Develop a comprehensive list of keywords and topics relevant to your brand, industry, and products. This includes branded terms, industry jargon, and specific product names. Social listening tools can then track and analyze conversations around these keywords.

4. Monitor Multiple Social Channels:

- Expand your social listening efforts across various social media channels, forums, blogs, and review sites. Customers express opinions and engage in discussions on diverse platforms, and monitoring multiple channels provides a holistic view of the online landscape.

5. Understand Customer Sentiment:

- Analyze customer sentiment expressed in social media conversations. By identifying positive, negative, or neutral sentiments, brands can gauge the overall perception of their products or services and respond promptly to potential issues.

6. Track Industry Trends and Competitor Activity:

- Extend social listening to monitor industry trends and keep tabs on competitor activities. Understanding broader market trends and the strategies of competitors can inform your brand's positioning and help identify areas for innovation.

7. Engage in Real-Time Crisis Management:

- Leverage social listening for real-time crisis management. By monitoring conversations, brands can quickly identify and address emerging issues or negative sentiments, minimizing the impact of potential crises on brand reputation.

8. Uncover Customer Pain Points and Needs:

- Dive deep into social conversations to identify customer pain points, needs, and expectations. Understanding the challenges and aspirations of your audience allows you to tailor products, services, and marketing strategies accordingly.

9. Identify Brand Advocates and Influencers:

- Identify and engage with brand advocates and influencers within your industry. Social listening helps discover individuals who actively promote your brand or have significant influence in your niche, allowing you to nurture relationships and potentially collaborate.

10. **Create Personalized Customer Experiences:**

- Use insights from social listening to enhance personalization in customer experiences. Tailor marketing messages, promotions, and product offerings based on the preferences and behaviors identified through social media conversations.

11. **Gather Feedback on Products and Services:**

- Actively seek and analyze customer feedback on products and services. Social listening provides a direct channel for customers to express their opinions, allowing brands to make data-driven improvements and innovations.

12. Segment and Analyze Audience Demographics:

- Social listening tools often offer demographic insights into your audience. Segment this data to understand the demographics of those discussing your brand. This information is valuable for targeted marketing and content creation.

13. Track Campaign Performance:

- Monitor the performance of marketing campaigns through social listening. Track mentions, sentiment, and audience engagement related to specific campaigns. Analyzing campaign performance allows for data-driven adjustments and optimizations.

14. Benchmark and Measure Brand Health:

- Establish benchmarks for key metrics and regularly measure the health of your brand through social listening. Monitoring trends over time provides a longitudinal perspective on customer sentiment and brand perception.

15. **Integrate Social Listening into Decision-Making:**

   - Integrate social listening insights into decision-making processes across departments. From marketing and product development to customer service and crisis management, social listening should inform and influence strategic decisions.

16. **Continuous Learning and Adaptation:**

   - Social media is dynamic, and customer sentiments evolve. Establish a culture of continuous learning and adaptation based on social listening insights. Regularly revisit your social listening strategy to align with evolving customer behaviors and industry trends.

In conclusion, leveraging social listening for customer insights is a strategic imperative for brands seeking to stay attuned to customer sentiments, preferences, and market dynamics. By tapping into the wealth of online conversations, brands can not only enhance their understanding of the customer journey but also position themselves as responsive and customer-centric entities in the ever-evolving digital landscape.

CHAPTER 5: INFLUENCER COLLABORATIONS AND PARTNERSHIPS

In the dynamic world of social media, influencers have emerged as powerful voices shaping trends, opinions, and consumer behaviors. "Influencer Collaborations and Partnerships" is a chapter dedicated to unraveling the intricacies of strategically aligning your brand with influential personalities to amplify your reach, engage your audience, and establish authentic connections.

As we delve into the realm of influencer collaborations, we'll explore the art of identifying the right influencers, crafting meaningful partnerships, and navigating the landscape of sponsored content. Join me on this journey as we uncover the strategies and insights that elevate influencer collaborations from mere transactions to authentic, mutually beneficial relationships. From micro-influencers to industry leaders, this chapter is a guide to harnessing the power of influencer marketing to not only expand your brand's visibility but also to create lasting impressions in the minds of your audience. Let's explore the nuances of influencer collaborations and partnerships, where the convergence of authenticity and strategic alignment propels brands to new heights in the digital era.

- Identifying and Approaching Relevant Influencers

In the expansive realm of social media, influencers have become instrumental in shaping consumer perceptions and driving brand engagement. Identifying and approaching relevant influencers is a strategic process that requires a deep understanding of your brand, target audience, and the influencer landscape. This comprehensive discussion explores the methodologies and best practices for successfully identifying and approaching influencers who align seamlessly with your brand.

1. **Define Your Objectives:**

   - Begin by clearly defining your influencer marketing objectives. Whether it's increasing brand awareness, driving sales, or promoting a specific campaign, having well-defined goals will guide your influencer selection process.

2. **Understand Your Target Audience:**

 - Gain a profound understanding of your target audience. Identify their demographics, interests, and preferred social media platforms. This knowledge is crucial for finding influencers whose followers align with your brand's target demographic.

3. **Research Relevant Niches and Industries:**

 - Conduct thorough research within your industry and related niches. Identify influencers who have a genuine and engaged following within these spaces. Collaborating with influencers already associated with relevant industries adds authenticity to your brand partnership.

4. **Utilize Influencer Marketing Tools:**

- Leverage influencer marketing tools to streamline your search. Platforms like Traackr, Hootsuite, and Influencity provide insights into influencer performance, audience demographics, and overall reach. These tools can facilitate a data-driven approach to influencer identification.

5. **Consider Micro-Influencers:**

- Don't overlook the impact of micro-influencers. While they may have a smaller following compared to macro-influencers, their audiences are often highly engaged and trusting. Micro-influencers can offer an authentic touch, particularly when targeting niche markets.

6. **Analyze Influencer Content Quality:**

- Scrutinize the quality and authenticity of an influencer's content. Evaluate the visual appeal, storytelling capability, and overall tone of their posts. Authentic and high-quality content resonates better with audiences and aligns more seamlessly with your brand.

7. Examine Engagement Metrics:

   - Look beyond follower count and assess engagement metrics. Influencers with a genuine connection to their audience often have higher engagement rates. Analyze likes, comments, shares, and overall interaction to gauge the influencer's impact.

8. Check Authenticity and Alignment:

   - Ensure that influencers align with your brand values and messaging. Authenticity is crucial; followers can easily discern when an influencer's partnership feels forced or incongruent with their usual content. Seek influencers whose personal brand aligns seamlessly with your brand identity.

9. Review Previous Collaborations:

   - Investigate an influencer's previous collaborations. Analyze the success of these partnerships and whether they align with your brand's goals. Assessing past collaborations provides insights into an influencer's professionalism, reliability, and effectiveness as a brand ambassador.

10. Evaluate Audience Demographics:

   - Examine the demographics of an influencer's audience. Ensure that their followers match your target demographic. Influencers with an audience that closely mirrors your ideal customer profile are more likely to drive meaningful engagement.

11. Assess Influencer Reputation:

   - Assess an influencer's reputation within the industry and among their followers. Check for any controversies, ethical concerns, or negative sentiments associated with the influencer. A positive and credible reputation is vital for a successful collaboration.

12. **Diversify Across Platforms:**

   - Consider influencers active across multiple platforms. Diversifying your influencer collaborations across platforms ensures broader reach and engagement. Influencers who excel on platforms like Instagram, YouTube, TikTok, or Twitter bring diverse audience segments into the fold.

13. **Personalized Outreach:**

   - Approach influencers with personalized and authentic outreach. Clearly articulate why you believe they are a great fit for your brand, referencing specific aspects of their content that resonate with your goals. Tailor your communication to each influencer individually.

14. **Negotiate Transparently:**

   - Approach negotiations with transparency. Communicate your expectations, deliverables, and compensation structure. A transparent approach fosters a positive working relationship and avoids misunderstandings during the collaboration.

15. **Provide Creative Freedom:**

   - Allow influencers creative freedom within the framework of your brand guidelines. Influencers have cultivated a specific style and tone that resonates with their audience. Providing creative freedom enhances authenticity and ensures that the collaboration feels organic.

16. **Build Long-Term Relationships:**

   - Foster long-term relationships with influencers. Successful influencer marketing is not just about one-off partnerships but establishing enduring connections. Building relationships over time contributes to consistent brand advocacy and trust.

In conclusion, the process of identifying and approaching relevant influencers requires a strategic blend of data-driven analysis, authenticity assessment, and targeted outreach. By aligning with influencers whose values and audience demographics resonate with your brand, you can forge meaningful collaborations that elevate your brand's visibility and engagement in the dynamic landscape of social media.

- Negotiating Successful Partnerships

Negotiating influencer partnerships is a delicate dance that requires finesse, clear communication, and a strategic approach. Crafting successful collaborations involves aligning expectations, determining fair compensation, and fostering a mutually beneficial relationship. This comprehensive discussion explores the key elements and best practices for negotiating successful influencer partnerships.

1. **Understand Your Objectives:**

   - Begin negotiations with a clear understanding of your campaign objectives. Whether it's increasing brand awareness, driving sales, or launching a new product, aligning objectives helps set the stage for a partnership that delivers measurable results.

2. **Define Key Performance Indicators (KPIs):**

   - Establish key performance indicators (KPIs) that align with your campaign goals. Whether you're measuring engagement, reach, conversions, or a combination of metrics, clearly define what success looks like for the influencer and your brand.

3. **Research Influencer Metrics:**

- Before negotiations, thoroughly research the influencer's metrics and performance. Analyze their engagement rates, audience demographics, and past campaign results. This data provides insights into the influencer's impact and aids in setting realistic expectations.

4. **Offer Fair Compensation:**

   - Compensation is a crucial aspect of negotiations. Research industry standards and ensure that your offer aligns with the influencer's reach, audience engagement, and overall impact. A fair compensation package fosters a positive and collaborative partnership.

5. **Consider Non-Monetary Benefits:**

   - In addition to monetary compensation, consider offering non-monetary benefits. This can include exclusive access to products, event invitations, or co-created content opportunities. Non-monetary perks enhance the overall value of the collaboration.

6. Clearly Define Deliverables:

- Clearly outline the deliverables expected from the influencer. This includes the number of posts, types of content (e.g., photos, videos, stories), and any specific messaging or brand guidelines. Clarity in expectations sets the foundation for a successful collaboration.

7. Determine Content Usage Rights:

- Clearly define content usage rights. Specify whether the brand has the right to repurpose influencer-created content for marketing purposes. Establishing these terms upfront avoids potential conflicts and ensures legal compliance.

8. Establish Timelines and Deadlines:

- Communicate timelines and deadlines for the campaign. Establish when content should be created, and published, and any key dates associated with the campaign. Timely execution is crucial for campaigns with specific launch or event schedules.

9. **Negotiate Exclusivity Agreements:**

- Discuss exclusivity agreements if applicable. Determine whether the influencer will be exclusive to your brand for a specific period. Exclusivity agreements prevent conflicts of interest and enhance the brand's association with the influencer.

10. **Include Performance-Based Incentives:**

- Consider incorporating performance-based incentives into the negotiation. For example, offer bonuses or additional compensation based on the achievement of specific performance milestones, such as reaching a certain engagement rate or driving a targeted number of conversions.

11. **Discuss Creative Freedom:**

- Address the level of creative freedom the influencer will have. While brand guidelines are essential, allowing influencers some creative autonomy often results in more authentic and engaging content. Strike a balance between brand messaging and the influencer's unique style.

12. **Clarify Revisions and Edits:**

   - Communicate the process for revisions and edits. Establish how feedback will be provided, the number of allowed revisions, and any specific requirements for content adjustments. Transparent communication in this area avoids misunderstandings during the collaboration.

13. **Ensure FTC Compliance:**

   - Discuss and ensure compliance with FTC guidelines. Collaborations should include proper disclosure of the influencer's relationship with your brand. This transparency is not only a legal requirement but also contributes to building trust with the audience.

14. **Address Long-Term Collaboration Possibilities:**

- If the initial partnership is successful, discuss the possibility of long-term collaborations. Building a lasting relationship with influencers can lead to consistent brand advocacy and ongoing engagement with their audience.

15. **Include Contingency Plans:**

- Anticipate potential challenges and include contingency plans in your negotiations. Discuss how unexpected situations, such as changes in campaign goals or influencer availability, will be addressed. Preparing for contingencies ensures smoother collaboration execution.

16. *Finalize in a Legally Binding Agreement:*

- Once negotiations are complete, formalize the terms in a legally binding agreement. Include all agreed-upon details, such as compensation, deliverables, timelines, and any exclusivity or usage rights. Having a written contract protects both parties and ensures a clear understanding of expectations.

In conclusion, negotiating successful influencer partnerships is an intricate process that requires a balance between the brand's goals and the influencer's unique voice. Clear communication, fair compensation, and a focus on mutual benefits contribute to collaborations that not only meet campaign objectives but also foster positive, long-term relationships between brands and influencers in the ever-evolving landscape of influencer marketing.

- Maximizing the Impact of Influencer Marketing

In the dynamic landscape of digital marketing, influencer collaborations have become a cornerstone for brands aiming to connect authentically with their target audience. Maximizing the impact of influencer marketing involves a strategic and comprehensive approach that goes beyond individual partnerships. This discussion explores key strategies and best practices for harnessing the full potential of influencer marketing to elevate brand visibility, engagement, and conversion rates.

1. **Define Clear Objectives:**

   - Start by defining clear objectives for your influencer marketing campaigns. Whether it's increasing brand awareness, driving website traffic, or boosting sales, having well-defined goals ensures that your efforts are aligned with measurable outcomes.

2. **Audience-Centric Approach:**

   - Tailor influencer collaborations to resonate with your target audience. Understand the demographics, interests, and preferences of your audience, and select influencers whose content aligns seamlessly with these characteristics. An audience-centric approach enhances the authenticity and relatability of your brand.

3. **Diversify Influencer Partnerships:**

   - Embrace diversity in your influencer partnerships. Collaborate with influencers across various niches, demographics, and platforms. Diversification ensures a broader reach and allows your brand to connect with different segments of your audience.

4. **Micro-Influencers for Niche Impact:**

   - Consider working with micro-influencers for niche impact. Micro-influencers often have highly engaged and loyal followers within specific niches. Their recommendations can carry significant weight and foster a sense of authenticity and trust.

5. **Leverage Cross-Platform Visibility:**

   - Capitalize on cross-platform visibility by collaborating with influencers active on multiple social media platforms. This approach ensures that your brand is exposed to diverse audiences with varying preferences for content consumption.

6. **Integrate Influencers into Campaigns:**

   - Integrate influencers seamlessly into your broader marketing campaigns. Whether it's a product launch, seasonal promotion, or a charitable initiative, incorporating influencers into your overall marketing strategy ensures cohesive messaging and enhances campaign impact.

7. Create Engaging and Authentic Content:

- Prioritize the creation of engaging and authentic content. Influencers are valued for their unique voice and storytelling abilities. Encourage creative freedom within brand guidelines to produce content that resonates with both the influencer's audience and your brand messaging.

8. Implement Tracking and Analytics:

- Utilize tracking and analytics tools to measure the performance of influencer campaigns. Monitor key metrics such as engagement rates, reach, and conversion data. Analyzing data provides insights into the effectiveness of your influencer marketing strategy and informs future decisions.

9. Encourage User-Generated Content (UGC):

- Foster user-generated content by encouraging followers to create content inspired by influencer collaborations. UGC not only amplifies the reach of your influencer campaigns but also showcases authentic interactions with your brand.

10. **Run Contests and Giveaways**:

- Enhance the impact of influencer marketing by running contests and giveaways in collaboration with influencers. This strategy boosts engagement, encourages user participation, and creates a sense of excitement around your brand.

11. **Invest in Long-Term Relationships:**

- Cultivate long-term relationships with influencers. Building ongoing partnerships fosters consistency in brand messaging, establishes brand loyalty among the influencer's audience, and often leads to more impactful collaborations over time.

12. **Activate Influencers as Brand Ambassadors:**

   - Elevate the impact of influencer marketing by activating influencers as brand ambassadors. Brand ambassadors go beyond individual campaigns; they embody the values and identity of your brand, contributing to sustained brand advocacy.

13. **Incorporate Influencers in Events:**

   - Integrate influencers into events, whether physical or virtual. Involve influencers in product launches, conferences, or exclusive brand experiences. Their presence can amplify event visibility and generate real-time engagement.

14. **Utilize Influencers in Educational Content:**

   - Collaborate with influencers to create educational content. Whether it's tutorials, how-to guides, or informative discussions, influencers can serve as credible sources of information and add value to your audience's experience.

15. Capitalize on Seasonal Trends and Holidays:

   - Leverage seasonal trends and holidays by incorporating influencers into relevant campaigns. Whether it's festive promotions, seasonal discounts, or themed content, aligning with influencers during peak periods maximizes the impact of your marketing efforts.

16. Measure and Optimize Continuously:

   - Continuously measure the performance of influencer campaigns and optimize based on insights. Analyze data, gather feedback, and refine your approach to ensure that each collaboration contributes to your overarching marketing goals.

In conclusion, maximizing the impact of influencer marketing involves a strategic combination of audience-centric planning, diverse collaborations, and integration into broader marketing initiatives. By fostering authentic connections, measuring campaign performance, and adapting to evolving trends, brands can harness the full potential of influencer marketing to create lasting impressions and drive meaningful engagement in the digital landscape.

- Measuring ROI and Evaluating Influencer Performance

The success of influencer marketing goes beyond the creative and engaging content produced; it hinges on the ability to measure Return on Investment (ROI) and evaluate influencer performance effectively. This comprehensive discussion delves into the key metrics, strategies, and tools necessary for accurately assessing the impact of influencer campaigns and ensuring that your marketing efforts align with business objectives.

1. **Establish Clear Objectives and KPIs:**

   - Begin by establishing clear objectives for your influencer marketing campaigns. Whether it's brand awareness, website traffic, or sales conversion, aligning objectives with Key Performance Indicators (KPIs) provides a framework for measuring success.

2. **Utilize Tracking and Analytics Tools:**

   - Leverage tracking and analytics tools to monitor influencer campaign performance. Platforms like Google Analytics, social media analytics tools, and dedicated influencer marketing platforms provide insights into reach, engagement, and conversion data.

3. **Track Engagement Metrics:**

   - Monitor engagement metrics to gauge the effectiveness of influencer content. Metrics such as likes, comments, shares, and click-through rates provide valuable insights into audience interaction and the resonance of the influencer's messaging.

4. **Measure Reach and Impressions:**

   - Assess the reach and impressions generated by influencer content. Platforms often provide data on the number of views, impressions, and unique users exposed to influencer posts. Understanding the reach helps quantify the visibility of your brand.

5. **Evaluate Follower Growth:**

   - Evaluate the growth in the influencer's follower count during and after the campaign. While a short-term spike in followers may occur during the campaign, sustained growth indicates a positive impact on the influencer's audience and potential long-term brand exposure.

6. **Track Website Traffic and Conversions:**

- Utilize UTM parameters and tracking links to monitor website traffic generated by influencer campaigns. Track conversions and sales attributed to influencer-driven traffic to measure the direct impact on your bottom line.

7. **Calculate Earned Media Value (EMV):**

- Calculate Earned Media Value (EMV) to quantify the value generated by influencer content. EMV assigns a monetary value to the exposure and engagement received, helping you assess the cost-effectiveness of your influencer marketing efforts.

8. **Assess Sentiment Analysis:**

- Conduct sentiment analysis to gauge the overall sentiment associated with influencer content.

Evaluate the ratio of positive to negative sentiments in comments and mentions to understand the impact on brand perception.

9. **Monitor Influencer-Generated Content:**

   - Track the performance of influencer-generated content beyond the initial campaign. Assess how well this content continues to engage audiences, whether through user-generated content, shares, or ongoing interactions.

10. **Compare Against Benchmarks:**

   - Benchmark influencer campaign performance against industry standards and previous campaigns. Comparing metrics against benchmarks provides context and allows you to identify areas of improvement or success.

11. **Evaluate Cross-Channel Impact:**

   - If the campaign involves multiple influencers across various platforms, evaluate the cross-channel impact. Assess how the campaign resonates differently on each platform and adapt future strategies accordingly.

12. Consider Long-Term Impact:

- Consider the long-term impact of influencer collaborations on brand loyalty and customer retention. Measure how influencer campaigns contribute to sustained engagement, repeat business, and the overall growth of your brand community.

13. Collect Feedback from Influencers:

- Gather feedback from influencers regarding their experience with the campaign. Insights from influencers can provide qualitative data on aspects such as the collaboration process, brand fit, and audience response.

14. Calculate Return on Ad Spend (ROAS):

- Calculate Return on Ad Spend (ROAS) by dividing the revenue generated by the influencer campaign by the total spend. ROAS provides a clear metric for understanding the monetary returns relative to the investment made in influencer marketing.

15. **Adjust Strategies Based on Insights:**

 - Adjust your influencer marketing strategies based on the insights gathered from campaign performance. Identify what worked well and areas for improvement, and incorporate these learnings into future collaborations.

16. **Use Surveys and Brand Lift Studies:**

 - Implement surveys and brand lift studies to measure the impact of influencer campaigns on brand awareness, perception, and purchase intent. These studies provide valuable data beyond immediate engagement metrics.

In conclusion, measuring ROI and evaluating influencer performance is a multifaceted process that requires a combination of quantitative and qualitative analyses. By leveraging analytics tools, tracking relevant metrics, and continuously adapting strategies based on insights, brands can ensure that influencer marketing efforts not only resonate with the audience but also contribute meaningfully to business objectives.

CONCLUSION

As we draw the curtains on "Top Tips for Growing Your Startup on Social Media," it's not just the end of a book but the beginning of a transformative journey for your startup. Navigating the dynamic landscape of social media is no longer a mere option but a strategic imperative for burgeoning businesses.

In our exploration, we've uncovered the fundamental principles that lay the groundwork for a robust social media strategy. From defining your brand identity and crafting compelling content to leveraging influencers and setting measurable goals, each chapter has been a stepping stone towards establishing a formidable online presence.

Remember, social media is not a one-size-fits-all solution. It's a canvas for creativity, innovation, and authentic connections. The tips shared are not rigid rules but guiding lights, encouraging you to infuse your startup's unique essence into every tweet, post, or story.

As your startup embarks on this social media odyssey, stay agile. The digital landscape evolves, and so should your strategies. Embrace new trends, adapt to changing algorithms, and most importantly, listen to your audience. Social media is a conversation, and your startup has a voice – make it resonate.

In the ever-expanding realm of startups, social media isn't just a tool; it's a vehicle for storytelling, community-building, and brand elevation. Your startup is more than a product or service; it's a narrative waiting to unfold. Through these top tips, I hope you've not only gained insights but also sparked a newfound enthusiasm to conquer the social media sphere.

As you implement these tips, track your progress, celebrate victories, and learn from challenges. Remember, every like, share, and comment is a testament to the impact your startup is making in the digital universe.

May your startup's journey on social media be filled with authenticity, engagement, and lasting connections. Here to the growth, success, and innovation that lie ahead. Go forth and conquer the social media landscape with the confidence that your startup is not just participating in a trend but shaping its destiny in the digital age. Cheers to the limitless possibilities that await your startup on the vibrant canvas of social media.